Unflattering Photos of Fascists

Authoritarianism in Trump's America

Edited by Christopher Ketcham
Photographs by Jeff Schwilk

AK Press
Chico

DISCLAIMER—PLEASE READ

The photographs you see in this book were all taken at public, right wing extremist events. The purpose is to capture the ethos of the demonstrations, not to characterize the ideology or affiliations of every person depicted in the photos, let alone label everyone depicted a fascist. Some of those present may instead be garden-variety patriot militia members, Islamophobes, incels, western chauvinists, simple MAGA hat heads, or even just 4chan LARPERS, etc. Some may have had reasons for showing up unrelated to any ideological or social identification with white nationalism or white supremacy. Some perhaps were just curious or blundered onto the scene. Others might have reformed their views since these photos were taken.

Whatever their reasons for being there, everyone depicted in these photographs put themself adjacent to displays of white nationalism, the rhetoric and politics of which are too toxic to ignore. It is not a good look for anyone present and participating.

Fascist ideology is notoriously complex. It is built on contradictions that make it highly adaptable. *Unflattering Photos of Fascists* is not meant to be a reference volume on contemporary fascism. There are trustworthy sources for this information. A good place to start is Shane Burley's *Fascism Today: What It is and How to End It* (2017).

For those curious about the fascist symbols on display, have a look at our glossary on page 36. There is certainly some clownish humor in these photographs. At the same time, our glossary should provide serious eye opening for anyone skeptical of the danger posed by white nationalists and white supremacists (and the gravity of cavorting alongside them).

AK Press
370 Ryan Ave. #100
Chico, CA 95973
www.akpress.org
akpress@akpress.org

Please contact us to request the latest AK Press distribution catalog, which features books, pamphlets, zines, and stylish apparel published and/or distributed by AK Press. Alternatively, visit our websites for the complete catalog, latest news, and secure ordering.

Unflattering Photos of Fascists
Authoritarianism in Trump's America

contents

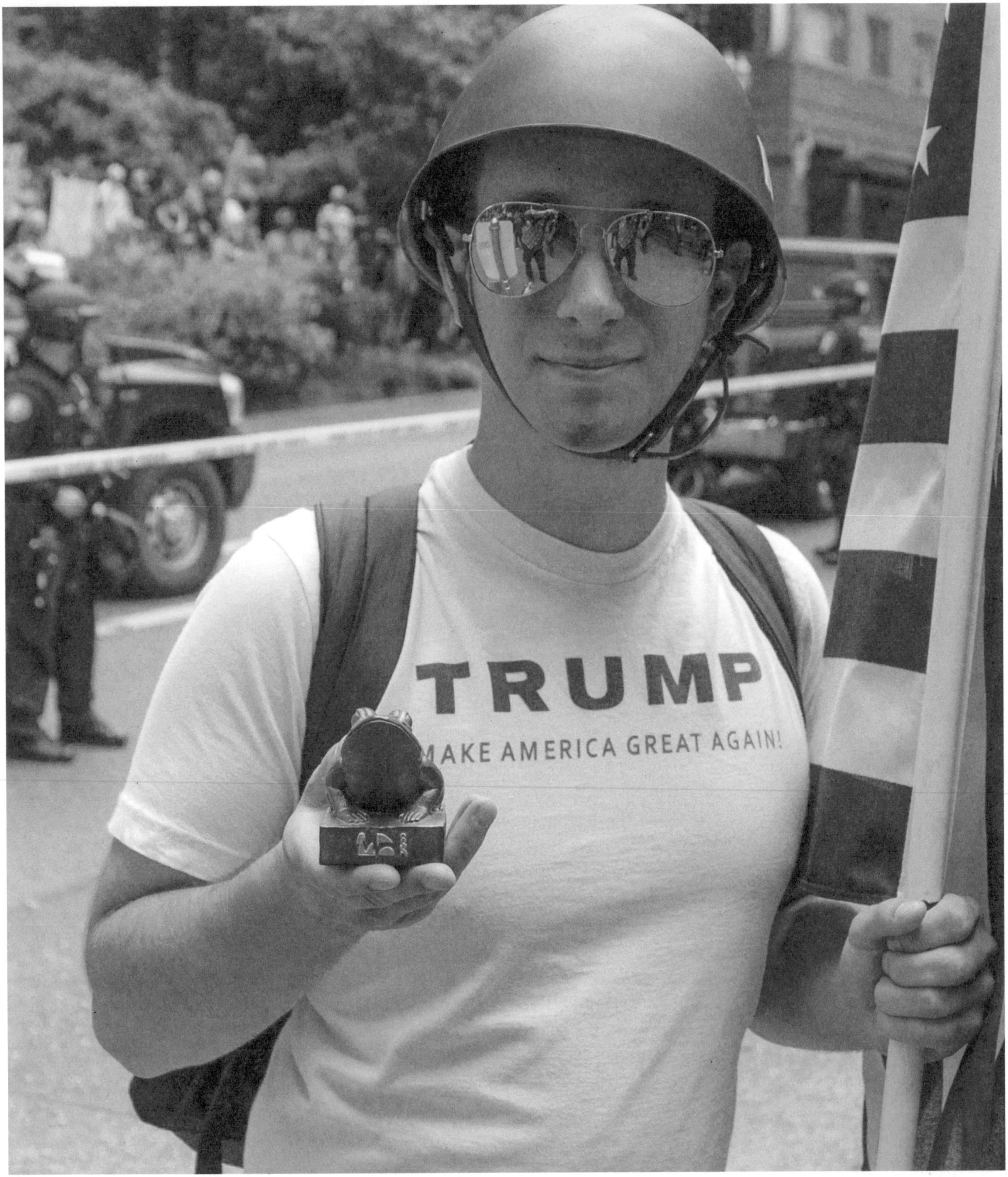
TRUMP
MAKE AMERICA GREAT AGAIN!

Introduction

▶ **Christopher Ketcham**

You are about to enter a world of people in a holy war. Their enemies are many. They are fighting against communists and socialists, and against multi-ethnic American integration, against the Democratic Party (for being a communist conspiracy), against people of color and immigrants infringing on white identity, against non-Christians (Muslims especially), against atheists, against liberals in cities, against yuppies and Jews and intellectuals and photographers like Jeff Schwilk. Kudos to Schwilk for immersing himself in this mob, trying to find some measure of humor in depicting what is otherwise a gallery of—for want of a better word—assholes.

For me it is a strange war they posit, a kind of fantasy war—one whose enemies don't quite exist. The enemies are not identified by the warriors in any way that actually describes reality. Their war has no relationship to the overwhelming existential crisis that now faces humanity, the crisis of the coming climate-change-driven ecological disruption that threatens civilization. They fight for an undefined and elusive "freedom." It's a petty, venal, purely individualistic freedom they seek. Always happy to tread on others despite what their flag says.

My prejudice as an environmental journalist, a prejudice which is perhaps my blind spot, is to spend time pondering the things that matter ultimately—our relationship with mother earth, the provider of all life, and whether the relationship will be gentle or vicious—and I forget that people have other motivations than ecology.

These beasts, gathered as a mob, might just murder us all given the chance.

The folks depicted in Schwilk's photographs are possibly good and kind in their personal lives, caring for their families, seeking something better for their children. But my guess is that, like most Americans, they don't give a rat's ass about the earth and its future and are simply thinking of the short term. In terms of ecological mindfulness, to call them "fascist" or "right wing" really doesn't distinguish them from the putative enemy on the other side of the political equation, i.e. the "left" or the Democratic Party. Democrats and Republicans, left and right, are united all in the delusion that the earth can and should be inexhaustibly exploited for the benefit of the one holy species, *Homo sapiens*, and with such a destructive imprint that it will likely lead to civilizational suicide.

The enormously important question of whether we will hand down a livable planet to our children is not one you will find asked among the people in Schwilk's gallery. It is not the matter at all. What I see depicted is stupid, blind, vicious selfishness. These are people with no understanding of political economy, no commitment to mutual aid, no understanding of ecology, no consciousness of humanity's all-important relations with the earth. And having no such understanding, they pose no threat to the capitalist system of economic growth.

What the dimwits want is simply more. And if it comes down to a choice of (1) more for us, the white chosen ones who are the more chosen of the chosen species, versus (2) sharing a little bit with the other less chosen of the chosen species—well, then crank up the hate, increase the inequality. You can die for my convenience. The earth can die, too.

Is this a materialistic and reductionist view of the "fascists" depicted? Perhaps. I am not a good judge of human beings. I subscribe to the school of the sacred scrolls in the film *Planet of the Apes*: "Beware the beast man, for he is the Devil's pawn. Alone among God's primates, he kills for sport or lust or greed. Yea, he will murder his brother to possess his brother's land. Let him not breed in great numbers, for he will make a desert of his home and yours."

I admit to great laughter at seeing the costumed ignoramuses parading, preening, and prancing about, and though I'm tempted to say that they are harmless, I think that would be a mistake. These beasts, gathered as a mob, might just murder us all given the chance. If mother nature doesn't get to us first. ◀

▶ Unflattering

▶ Photos of

▶ Fascists.

Visual Glossary of Fascist Symbols

▶ **Jeff Schwilk**

Cascade Legion: a "fighting formation" whose stated goal is to provide defense to the right wing and assist the police while engaging in political repression of their opponents (antifascists). They are based in the Puget Sound area of the Pacific Northwest. Their membership varies from Internet meme enthusiasts, actual neo-nazis, Odinists, and fascist heathens.

RWDS (Right-Wing Death Squad): an Alt Right, Internet-based fantasy of a death squad, which removes anything "degenerate" and seen as a threat to the state, through firing squads, lynching, and other brutal killing methods. RWDS is often associated with Moonman who have a song titled "Right Wing Death Squads" in which they talk about killing Black and Jewish People. RWDS is a meme making fun of leftist hysteria about imminent fascist doom.

RWSS (Right-Wing Safety Squad): a far-right online group that formed in the wake of the tragic "Ghostship Fire" in Oakland, CA. This group claimed that all "artspaces and illegal venues" were "hotbeds of liberal radicalism and degeneracy," and requested others to report any code violations in an effort to "Make America Safe Again." This group uses the same double lightning bolt runes (SS) that the Nazi paramilitary organization used. Even the name, Safety Squad, elicits comparisons to the Nazi's Schutzstaffel, which translates to "protection squadron." After the eviction of the popular Richmond, CA, DIY venue "Burnt Ramen," Mayor Tom Butt initially wrote on his website that he was alerted to purported code violations by a "social media author," but later retracted that statement, saying it was an email from a concerned resident.

Odal Rune/NSM (National Socialist Movement): This rune replaced the swastika on the uniforms and banners of the NSM after the inauguration of Donald Trump. This was done as a way to "mainstream" the organization and more effectively connect with the growing American nationalist movement. Founded in 1974, this group has its roots in the American Nazi Party. Until recently, the NSM was the largest organized neo-nazi group in the US. Members of this group were some of the main organizers of the 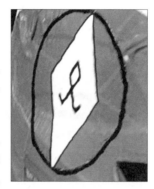 August 2017 "Unite the Right Rally" in Charlottesville, VA, and were subsequently targeted in a series of federal and state lawsuits which focused on prosecuting civil rights violations and the illegal usage of militia forces to protect Alt Right and white nationalist demonstrations. In early 2019, the director and president of the NSM, Jeff Shoep, turned over leadership to James Hart Stern, a Black activist who vowed to destroy the NSM from the inside. Shoep hoped that by doing so he would avoid legal responsibility for the NSM's role in Charlottesville. Currently, the NSM seems to have lost many members and is now more or less inactive.

 **Hoppean Snake/Chilean Dictator Augusto Pinochet**: The Hoppean snake cartoon is a direct reference to Hans Hermann Hoppe, an Austrian anarcho-capitalist who advocates the physical removal from society of communists, homosexuals, environmentalists, and anyone he deems outside the norm. This cartoon snake often accompanies the phrase "Free Helicopter Rides" and depictions of former Chilean dictator Augusto Pinochet. All of these memes reference "death flights," the practice of throwing political opponents from helicopters during Pinochet's regime between 1973 and 1990. Right-wing extremists use this meme to "joke" about executing their political opponents. Over forty thousand actual and suspected dissidents lost their lives during Pinochet's brutal reign.

Kekistan Flag: A German Nazi War flag, with the Kek logo replacing the swastika and the green replacing the infamous German red. Kek originates from the online game "World of Warcraft" in which certain characters' conversations are rendered in a cryptic form of script based on Korean; thus, the common chat phrase "LOL" (laugh out loud) was read by opposing players as "KEK." The phrase caught on as a variation on "LOL" in game chat rooms. Kek is also a frog-headed Egyptian god of chaos and darkness, which happens to fit perfectly with the Alt Right's self-image as primarily devoted to destroying the existing world order. Members of the far right are particularly fond of the way the banner trolls the opposition who recognize its nazi origins.

OK Hand Signal: In 2015, various Alt Right members/Trump supporters began using this seemingly innocuous hand signal, and it has been associated with the far right since then. In 2017, an anonymous 4Chan user started an online campaign (Operation O-KKK) to obfuscate the use of the OK sign as a far-right dog-whistle and instead make it only look like a symbol to "troll the libs." Over the years, people across a broad swath of the populace, including cops, Trump administration officials, and conservative students have all 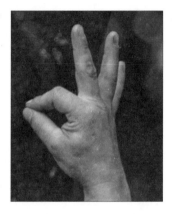 used this hand signal while denying they are white supremacists. Even if they are not avowed racists, though, people who make this gesture are signaling that they are "OK" with others thinking they are racists for the sake of a joke. It's pretty hard to insist you're not a racist when you are trying to trick people into thinking you are one.

Confederate Heritage: Based on the battle flag of General Lee's Army of Northern Virginia flown by states with enslaved people during the American Civil War. After the War it became a symbol of rebel pride. In the early-twentieth century, it was adopted by the Ku Klux Klan as the Klan waged a white-supremacist campaign of terror against the Black population. Segregationists

widely flaunted the Confederate symbol during the anti-segregation fights of the 1950s and 1960s. Around the same time, state and municipal governments began flying the Confederate flag over state capitols and city halls across the South. A symbol of slavery and white supremacy, the Confederate flag remains in wide use by white supremacist and fascists in the United States and abroad, as a potent symbol of racial hatred and oppression.

Boogaloo (also known as The Big Igloo, Big Luau, The Boogaloo Bois): An anti-government arm of the patriot militia movement that seeks to foment civil war in the United States. The name "Boogaloo" derives from a joke about a second civil war combined with the title of the 1980s breakdancing film *Breakin' 2: Electric Boogaloo.* The Boogaloo movement got its start on 4chan on the /k/ weapons board. It later went mainstream  through Facebook. Its adherents signify their allegiance by wearing Hawaiian shirts in public. They garnered widespread awareness at the January 20, 2020 pro-gun demonstration in Virginia, and again a few months later during the "open the lockdown" demonstrations around the United States against the COVID-19 pandemic quarantine orders. Boogaloo adherents also made appearances during the Justice for George Floyd rebellions across the country in May and June 2020. ◀

Disarming the Fascists, with Photography

▶ **Jeff Schwilk**

Olympia, WA, August 9th, 1992. It was a pleasant summer day. I was a nineteen-year-old skate-punk recently returned from my first year at college, and the world seemed a place of joyous adventure.

My friends and I had been skateboarding around downtown, and late in the afternoon we decided to take a breather on the steps of the gazebo in our favorite spot to relax, Sylvester Park. We chatted about skating and upcoming punk shows. One of the folks in the park that afternoon was Bob Buchanan, an infamous teen-aged gutter punk who had lived on the streets of Olympia since the age of thirteen and who was known for being drunk, violent, and generally out of control.

One particularly gruesome story about him involved his attack on a young pregnant woman. Apparently, Bob beat her to the ground so badly that she nearly lost consciousness. In an attempt to hold Bob accountable, a locally distributed zine described this incident and warned readers in the punk community that Bob was "a nazi" and someone to avoid. Bob, who was mixed ethnicity of Thai and Caucasian parents, lived a brutal existence and was an angry kid, but I knew he wasn't a nazi. He had a history of partying with skinheads, some of whom *were* nazis, but always remained outspoken about his antifascist beliefs—which often led to him being assaulted by these racists.

I did not know Bob well, but he once confided in me that he had done many bad things and wanted to change his life, get off the streets, find a job, make a better life for himself. He also told me of numerous recent encounters that he experienced with fascists whom he now believed were stalking him.

Around sunset, two skinheads came into the park carrying a case of beer. They approached our group and claimed to be SHARPs (Skinheads Against Racial Prejudice) from Orange County, California. Their story was that they had traveled up the coast searching for nazi skinheads to beat up and were headed

to Seattle. They asked our group if anyone wanted to go drink beer with them. The majority of us declined, feeling uncertain about the strangers, but a few, including Bob, accompanied them.

After about forty-five minutes, everyone except Bob and the skinheads returned. According to those who had gone drinking, they had partied in a train tunnel on the edge of downtown. One of the strangers had spiderwebs tattooed on his head—a common nazi tattoo—and he repeatedly boasted of recent violent encounters.

My passion is birds, and most of my photographic work has not been about rightwing lunatics but about the beauty and splendor of avians.

My friends and I decided it was time to get out of there. Since Bob often hung out with sketchy skinheads and loved to drink, we didn't think much about leaving without him. Just as the twelve of us were piling into a small pick-up truck, the skinheads returned carrying another case of beer and asked if we wanted to return to the train tunnel and drink. We refused, and as the pick-up pulled away the skinheads chased after the truck, shouting, "Oi Oi Oi!" This was the last I would see of them.

The next day I went to work at the dry cleaner where I was a delivery driver. That morning's *Olympian*, the local newspaper, had a frontpage photo of police standing arounde a corpse clad in a leather jacket and combat boots. I immediately knew it was Bob. Word on the street was that his body had been found in the tunnel, mutilated almost beyond recognition.

Apparently, after our departure, the skinheads, later identified as Mark Gustafson and Gerald Rapali, returned to Bob at the train tunnel and continued to drink with him. As they all grew more intoxicated, the skinheads became belligerent and began asking Bob if he was a nazi, to which he replied, "Fuck no! I hate nazis!" They responded—surprise!—that *they* were nazis. A confrontation ensued in which the skinheads disarmed of his knife a now very drunk Bob and used it to attack him, stabbing him multiple times until he stopped moving. They then bludgeoned him with a broken parking meter, and finally dropped a boulder on his head, shattering his skull.

Following this horrific assault, the skinheads drank more beer then left Olympia. Driving south on Interstate 5, they stopped at a convenience store in the small town of Grand Mound. Inside the store, the skinheads got into a confrontation with a couple of locals. The locals retreated to their vehicle while the skinheads retrieved an SKS assault rifle from the trunk of their car. They fired multiple shots into the locals' vehicle as they fled, killing an innocent bystander who happened

to be napping in the back of their car. This was the end of the skinheads' rampage. They were arrested and ultimately plead guilty to both murders.

This incident transformed me. Quite suddenly, as if seeing and understanding the threat for the first time, I became aware of the presence of militant, murderous fascists all around me. Downtown Olympia suddenly seemed menacing. I became paranoid; I feared that someone was stalking *me*. On a number of occasions while riding my bicycle, strange vehicles seemed to be following me. There were also calls to my house in the late hours from unknown, blocked numbers, the callers saying nothing, sitting on the line, breathing.

One morning six months later, outside of my family's home in Olympia, I found my car vandalized, the windshield smashed in, and swastikas painted on the hood along with the words "white power" and "poser." I spoke with Bill Wassmuth of the Northwest Center Against Malicious Harassment and he informed me of a growing white supremacist movement in the South Puget Sound area. He also relayed rumors that there had been a plot to assassinate Bob by local white supremacists. I became set on trying to thwart this threat in any way I could, doing my own research and attempting to document signs of it. This book is part of that years-long effort.

By the mid-nineties, I had become heavily involved in the anarcho-punk scene in the Pacific Northwest, organizing for the WTO protests during the 1999 Battle of Seattle, battling against the timber industry across the region and against neoliberal economic policies in general. This sent me regularly into the streets with my comrades to challenge the status quo.

The punk scene during the 1990s was vibrant with underground activity and grassroots community building. Many of us travelled by freight train, subsisted on dumpster diving, squatted abandoned buildings, planted and tended community gardens, cooked meals for the homeless, published zines, sent books to prisoners, made street theater, and created music and art. Not uncommonly, nazi skinheads targeted us and, on a few occasions, clashes occurred.

On one memorable night, the renowned speed metal band Exodus was playing at a bar in Portland called EJ's. As this was the first time in twenty years the band had come to Portland—and they would be playing their entire first album, *Bonded by Blood*, with the original lead singer, Paul Baloff—it seemed like all the band's fans had come out of the woodwork. The small venue was packed, most of the floor was

The viewer gets a sense of an ultra-nationalist militia comic-con event verging on the ridiculous.

occupied by a very violent mosh pit, and there was almost no refuge from the melee. As soon as Exodus began their set, the crowd went crazy, ecstatically screaming the words to each song, a swirling mass of energy. It was an incredible show, but three songs into it a nazi skinhead from the audience jumped on stage and yelled "White Power!" into the mic. A few people in the crowd responded with a sieg heil. This continued through the rest of the show with more and more of the audience sieg heiling, until it seemed most of the crowd were making the fascist salute.

My friends and I were revolted at this display and came to the realization that we were surrounded by nazis and that our best bet was to leave before the show ended. We made our escape as the last song played. A few nazi skinheads were milling about in front of the venue. As my friends and I were greatly outnumbered, we quietly snuck away down the street to a nearby punk-friendly house. Word had gone out on an antifascist phone tree, however, that a large group of fascists were at EJ's, and within minutes at least twenty antifascists showed up ready for a fight. Unfortunately, they were outnumbered by the nazis, and after a violent clash they retreated and let the fascists go on their way. These sorts of encounters happened often enough that they became an indelible part of my experience.

Twenty years later, now a photojournalist, I have aimed my lens at members of far-right groups. One of the documentary projects I have undertaken involves coverage of the January 2016 takeover of the Malheur National Wildlife Refuge in eastern Oregon by an armed group of far-right extremists led by a self-described Mormon prophet named Ammon Bundy. Bundy's incursion there was personally offensive to me, as the Malheur National Wildlife Refuge holds a special place in my heart. My passion is birds, and most of my photographic work has not been about right-wing lunatics but about the beauty and splendor of avians. Malheur and the surrounding wildlands, home to a tremendous diversity of both resident and migrant avians, are a birdwatcher's Shangri-la in the Pacific Northwest.

The stand-off was yet another incident in the long war by extractors to privatize the public lands of the West and open them to more industrial for-profit exploitation. Once Ammon Bundy and his supporters stormed the refuge headquarters, the national media circus converged on the nearby town of Burns. I stayed at a hotel in Burns, the rooms of which were almost entirely taken up by members of the Idaho Three Percenters along with numerous right-wing media personalities who came to bask in the glory of Ammon's heroic takeover of federal land. I met members of

The punk scene during the 1990s was vibrant with underground activity and grassroots community-building.

The Center for Biological Diversity who were there protesting—and thus clashing with—the occupiers and their allies. The occupation lasted forty-one days. Many of the occupiers were convicted of various federal charges, but the leaders, Ammon Bundy, his brother Ryan, and seven others, managed to secure acquittals from a federal jury that appeared sympathetic to their cause. Upon hearing of this shocking development, I knew that the country had become a different place and that the upcoming election might bring a dreadful surprise: a Trump win.

As Trump took power and members of the far-right began clashing more often, and in more violent ways, with the antifascist movement in Portland, where I now live, I wanted to capture the pageantry and madness of our times. My technique has been to use longer lenses than the typical photographer at these events. This has allowed me to capture candid moments.

The photos show a surface clownishness. Many of the participants seem to imagine they inhabit a world in which they are superheroes, medieval knights, warriors for what they believe is the good and the true, clad in capes, armor, and helmets. Their pageantry sometimes leads to violence. Often it begins with taunting from either counter-protesters or the fascists themselves. Punches are thrown, pepper spray flies, and all hell breaks loose. In the photos from the demonstrations in downtown Portland, the viewer gets a sense of an ultra-nationalist militia comic-con event verging on the ridiculous.

The figure of the frog is an especially common symbol of today's neo-fascists. It references one of their mascots, the Internet meme Pepe the Frog, who is said to be the modern incarnation of the Egyptian god of chaos, Kek, a frog-headed humanoid. Stuffed animal frogs, small statues of Kek, and posters depicting Pepe are all on display, along with the flag of the imaginary nation of Kekistan. The Kekistan flag is a German Nazi regimental design with the swastika replaced by a series of Ks, serving as a symbol of one's alignment with neo-fascism. Additionally, these folks like to brandish depictions of anti-communist propaganda of the Cold War era, including signs celebrating Augusto Pinochet and other brutal dictators. And of course they are festooned with Trump banners, flags, and MAGA hats. Members of openly white-supremacist groups—Identity Evropa, Cascade Legion, Traditionalist Worker's Party, Patriot Front—have opportunized these events to recruit new members. Other groups such as Patriot Prayer, Proud Boys, and the Three Percenters claim not to organize with white supremacists, but in fact there is much overlap between these various groups.

Members of openly white-supremacist groups have opportunized these events to recruit new members.

They flaunt a thin veneer of multi-racialism, but an underlying fascist/ultra-nationalist ideology unites them. Rarely do they display any blatant symbols of white supremacy in public, but their expressions online are replete with extreme racist, homophobic, misogynistic, and anti-Semitic sentiments.

White supremacists have also embraced the gun rights movement, as part of their disturbing trend toward agitating for a "second civil war" or "Boogaloo," during which the enemies of the right will be exterminated by death squads clad in Hawaiian shirts (again, it all sounds ridiculous), and any challenge to the growing power of the right will be met by armed militias in the streets. When a newly elected Democratic governor took office in Virginia in 2018 and the legislature passed a number of gun regulation laws, a coalition of armed gun enthusiasts converged on the capitol two years later, numbering upwards of twenty thousand, many prepping for the Boogaloo. I spent time with these folks for this book as well.

The photos included may depict the subjects looking ridiculous. It would be easy to dismiss them as fools harmlessly enacting a fantasy. But core white supremacists are as deadly serious today as they have been throughout the country's history. Future oppressors are often viewed as bumbling idiots. But if we are too complacent, hindsight may show *us* to be the fools, blind to the threat.

The world has changed as the COVID-19 virus has swept across the country. The majority of the populace has followed the "shelter-in-place" orders instituted by state governments to slow the spread of the virus, but a significant percentage of the neo-fascist movement has used the lockdown as an excuse to organize rallies in opposition to what, in their eyes, are draconian measures to curb their freedom. These rallies have included MAGA cultists, 2nd Amendment/Gun-rights Activists, Anti-vaxxers, Three Percenters, anti-abortionists, Qanon true-believers, those anxious about the economy, Proud Boy crews, and the heavily armed neo-fascist/Boogaloo enthusiasts, all crowded closely together, most lacking PPE. The most disturbing aspect of these rallies has been a sort of normalization of the radical far-right/neo-fascists by the mainstream right-wing. Elderly FOX news viewers and other members of the general public can be seen taking selfies with the heavily armed neo-fascists who are clad in fascist insignia and symbols, smiling for the camera. Because there has been little or no resistance at such rallies, these disparate groups have been able to effectively organize and proselytize. The prospect of an uncertain future has surely drawn many new recruits to the far-right. It remains to be seen if this new coalition manages to stay unified. ◀

Future oppressors are often viewed as bumbling idiots. But if we are too complacent, hindsight may show us to be the fools, blind to the threat.

The Trumpenvolk

by Paul Street

As we sit at once mesmerized and sickened by the nonstop horror show staged by the terrible tiny-fingered tangerine-tinted Twitter-tantruming truth-trashing tyrant Trump, it is all too easy to forget that the repulsive Trump administration would not be possible without his dedicated followers. Trump is unimaginable without his millions of mostly white minions—a neofascistic cohort whose threat will live on past Trump's fall from power and perhaps someday back a more dedicated, zealous, and competent white-nationalist strongman than the narcissistic buffoon. The Trumpenvolk have stuck by their Dear Leader come hell or high water, consistent with candidate Trump's claim that his fans would stay with him even if he shot someone standing in the middle of Fifth Avenue.

As his impending impeachment and other controversies dominated headlines and haunted Trump's presidency at the end of November 2019, a majority of Republicans told *Economist* and YouGov pollsters that Trump was a better leader than former president Abraham Lincoln. The *Economist*/YouGov poll found that 87 percent of those in the GOP approved of the job the orange monstrosity was doing as president.[1]

"Trump," the senior administration official "Anonymous" wrote in the fall of 2019, "has been prone to misstatements as long as he's been in the public eye.... The problem is that people believe what he says because he's president."[2]

---

1 Kathy Frankovis, YouGov, December 2, 2019, https://today.yougov.com/topics/politics/articles-reports/2019/12/02/greatest-republican-president.
2 Anonymous, *A Warning* (New York: Twelve, 2019), 194.

If Trump says or tweets that a constitutional inquiry into his conduct is a treasonous "witch-hunt" led by "Radical Left Democrats," then the Trumpenvolk—the incestuous and hyper-partisan bias-confirming right-wing echo-chamber and noise and news machine (FOX News, right-wing talk radio, right-wing Twitter and Facebook networks, Breitbart, et al.), and their fans and minions—make it true in their minds. If Trump says/tweets that corporate neoliberals are socialist or even fascists, then the Trumpevolk agree. If Trump says/tweets that climate change is a hoax disseminated to weaken America and destroy jobs, then the Trumpenvolk internalize the claim as truth. If Trump says/tweets that the way to respond to school shootings is to arm teachers, then the Trumpenvolk concur. If Trump says/tweets that Central Americans desperately seeking to legally escape violence and poverty are really criminals seeking to invade and harm US citizens, then the Trumpenvolk fan the flames. If the monumentally corrupt oligarch and plutocrat Trump tells his supporters that he has put "the people" in power and cleaned up the corrupt swamp that rules the country on behalf of the nation's unelected dictatorship of money, then the Trumpenvolk say "yes master, thank you master!"

The Trumpenvolk are unfazed by evidence of their angry hero's sleazy depravity and boundless mendacity. Tell them that Trump serves multi-millionaires and billionaires, members of a capitalist ruling class that has profited immeasurably from Trump's tax cuts and deregulation, and they will denounce you as a communist. Tell them that Trump is committing Ecocide (the biggest crime of any and all time) by denying and escalating anthropogenic (really capitalogenic) climate change (the effort to turn the entire planet into a giant greenhouse gas chamber), they'll inform you that "climate change is a hoax" meant to "destroy jobs" and "weaken America."[3] Tell them that Joe Biden, Pete Buttigieg, Amy Klobuchar, Nancy Pelosi, Adam Schiff, Cory Booker, Charles Schumer, Barack Obama, and the Clintons are deeply conservative corporate-centrist neoliberals, not "radical Left" at all, they'll call you a "Low IQ" idiot who has been brainwashed by "the left-wing media." Tell them that two plus two equals four and they'll shake their heads in amazement at your gullibility.

The lockstep support that the ever-more white-nationalist-neofascist Republican Party's white-Amerikaner base and the Orwellian right-wing media give Trump is

> If Trump says/tweets that corporate neoliberals are socialist or even fascists, then the Trumpevolk agree.

---

3   Jason W. Moore, "Name the System: The Anthropocenes and the Capitalocene Alternative," *World-Ecological Imaginations*, October 9, 2016, https://jason-wmoore.wordpress.com/tag/capitalocene/.

why not a single Republican in the House of Representatives could bring themself to vote to impeach him for setting the United States' Founders' wigs on fire by trading military support to Ukraine for political dirt on Joe Biden.[4] Fear of white hot backlash from Trump's angry devotees and the highly propagandistic and confirmation-biasing right-wing noise/news machine and anti-social media they rely on for political information is why it was unthinkable that any but a few Republican Senators might vote to remove Trump from office for UkraineGate, much less for any of his other more substantial and vicious crimes against America and humanity.

It was unthinkable that any but a few Republican Senators might vote to remove Trump from office for UkraineGate, much less for any of his other more substantial and vicious crimes.

Fascists

Who is this Trump base and what is it all about? Like the proverbial broken clock that tells the time accurately twice a day, the dismal and deplorable dollar-Democrat Hillary Clinton got it right when she impolitically called Trump's backers "a basket of deplorables." The label is accurate, but it lacks the historical and sociopolitical precision of the more accurate terms "fascist" and "neofascist."

The Yale philosophy professor Jason Stanley, a descendant of Nazi Holocaust victims, drilled down into the key narrative components of fascist politics and ideology in his 2017 book *How Fascism Works*. Canvassing a broad history, Stanley lists the following top ten characteristics of a fascist-style politics and ideology past and present:

1) Constant propaganda to mask objectionable goals with the cloak of widely accepted ideals.
2) Fairytale notions of a glorious but betrayed national past—a lost golden age undermined by evil elites—of patriarchal racial purity.
3) Relentless attacks on intellectuals, expertise, and reasoned public discourse.
4) "Unreality": an assault on the public's capacity to perceive reality and "agree on truth."

---

4 Robert Reich, "Would the Founding Fathers Impeach Trump?" *American Prospect*, November 7, 2019, https://prospect.org/impeachment/would-the-founding-fathers-impeach-trump/.

5) The promotion and glorification of traditional social and political hierarchy.

6) The ubiquitous notion of ethnic and national victimhood.

7) A gospel of "law and order" linked to the criminalization of minorities.

8) Sexual anxiety connected to the charge of rape and the fear of ethnic inter-breeding and race-mixing.

9) "Sodom and Gomorrah": A rural and folkish, small-town suspicion of big cosmopolitan cities and their mysteriously diverse and morally suspect inhabitants.

10) Glorification of hard work, connected to the charges that the poor and minorities are lazy and dependent on welfare, that unions encourage laziness, and that intellectuals don't do real work.[5]

Beyond Stanley's list, we might also include related and overlapping trademark features of historical fascism: assaults on the rule of law; rejection of constitutional and parliamentary checks and balances; a Social Darwinian fixation on struggle, triumph/defeat, "thriving"/failing, strength/weakness, and superiority/inferiority; attacks on the free press; cults of personality; militarism; glorification of violence; the embrace of violence against political enemies and critics; the dehumanization of racial, ethnic, religious, cultural Others and political enemies; emotionally potent theatricality and extreme statements ("the greatest ever," "the worst ever," "amazing," "horrible," "tremendous," and so on); recurrent menacing rallies; belief in the superiority of instinct and will over reason and thought; the purging of the disloyal; a false posture of populism that cloaks service to and alliance with capitalist elites and capitalism; fierce anti-socialism; the worship of youth; the demonization and false conflation of liberals and "the Left"; and a predilection for bizarre conspiracy theories like the notions that the Jewish Elders of Zion and George Soros are secretly controlling world events.[6]

Trumpism overlaps fascism, past and present, enough to read it as part of the rising global twenty first century "populist" nationalist-neofascist movement that Trump's political guru and advisor Steve Bannon is working to foment around the world. Beneath his virulent narcissism and endless oligarchic corruption, the

Trump has worked to gather white "heartland" support with a toxic brew of hyper-militarism, immigrant-bashing nativism, law-and-order racism, sexism, and anti-intellectualism.

---

5   Jason Stanley, *How Fascism Works: The Politics of Us and Them* (New York: Random House, 2018).

6   Curt Guyette, "Is Trump a Fascist? The F-Word," *Detroit Metro Times*, September 11, 2019, https://www.metrotimes.com/detroit/is-trump-a-fascist/Content?oid=22617920&fbclid=IwAR0et8NBmnvDiji9ymmWRqmS4iWpuEsy2spxe8JO32y2oRqqWirYbJ2oVIM.

The widely documented parallels between Trumpism and fascism go beyond politics and ideology into the demographic composition of Trump's base.

Twitter and rally master Trump has worked to gather white "heartland" support with a toxic brew of hyper-militarism, immigrant-bashing nativism, law-and-order racism, sexism, and anti-intellectualism. Like Hitler in the early–middle 1930s, Trump has used "them and us" scapegoating to demonize "others," especially foreigners—such as Muslims, Mexican immigrants, "China," and other targets (e.g. Canadian timber exporters!)—to divert popular attention from his service to the rich and powerful. Like other fascists across history, he channels the "palingenetic nationalist" notion of a special, pure, national past ("Make America Great Again") which he claims cosmopolitan elites have betrayed.[7] He relentlessly assaults truth in ways both large and small, misrepresenting and twisting reality at an astonishing pace. The Trumpian assault on reason, intellectuals, law, democracy, parliamentarianism, a free press, the poor, science, decency, social justice, the common good, world peace, equality, and more has been relentless. In these and other ways, Trumpism is a close and consistent match with the hallmark characteristics of fascism as elucidated by a significant number of careful scholars.

The Myth of Trump as a Working-Class Hero

The widely documented parallels between Trumpism and fascism go beyond politics and ideology into the demographic composition of Trump's base. Like other fascist movements, past and present, Trumpism finds its main electoral support base primarily in the petite bourgeoisie, even while it mostly serves the interests of ruling-class corporate and finance capital. As the brilliant and historically astute eco-Marxist political sociologist John Bellamy Foster noted five months after the election:

> Who forms [the] social base of the neofascist [Trump] phenomenon? As a Gallup analysis and CNN exit polls have demonstrated, Trump's electoral support came mainly from the intermediate strata of the population, i.e., from the lower middle class and privileged sections of the working class, primarily those with annual household incomes above the median level of around $56,000… Trump's backing comes primarily neither from the working-class majority nor the capitalist class—though the latter have mostly reconciled themselves to Trumpism, given that they are its principal beneficiaries.[8]

---

7 Roger Griffin, *Fascism* (New York: Oxford University Press, 1995).
8 John Bellamy Foster, "Neofascism in the White House," *Monthly Review*, April 2017, https://monthlyreview.org/2017/04/01/neofascism-in-the-white-house/.

According to a mainstream media myth shared by intellectuals who ought to know better, Trump rode into the White House on a great upsurge of support from poor, white working-class voters drawn to the Republican candidate's "populist" anti-Wall Street pitch in key deindustrialized battleground states. This conventional "Rust Belt rebellion" wisdom was pronounced on the front page of the nation's newspaper of record, *The New York Times*, one day after the election. The *Times* proclaimed that Trump's victory was "a decisive demonstration of power by a largely overlooked coalition of mostly blue-collar white and working-class voters." *Times* political writer Nate Cohn decreed that *"Donald J. Trump won the presidency by riding an enormous wave of support among working-class whites"* (emphasis added).[9]

This storyline—repeated over and over and taken for granted in the mainstream media and even by much of the progressive left—is flatly contradicted by the data. As left political scientist Anthony DiMaggio noted seven months after the election, reviewing the relevant post-election polling data, Trump's support was "largely concentrated among more affluent Americans. Trump voters were significantly more likely to be older, white, Republican conservatives—a group that has been quite privileged historically speaking."[10] Further:

> Trump voters were not more likely to be unemployed, compared to non-Trump voters. Income-wise, the single largest group of Trump supporters was comprised of individuals hailing from households earning incomes of more than $100,000 a year—which made up 35 percent of all his voters. Those earning between $75,000 to $100,000 a year accounted for 19 percent of Trump voters, meaning that 54 percent of the president's supporters came from households earning over $75,000 a year. Another 20 percent of Trump supporters earned between $50,000 to $75,000 a year, putting them over the national median household income, which has long hovered around $50,000. In sum, approximately three-quarters of Trump voters were from households earning more than the national median income, while just one-quarter earned less than the median.

Like fascist and other right-nationalist political movements of the past, Trump has drawn his main support from the more reactionary segments of the middle class and petite bourgeoisie and the more privileged and well-off sections of the working-class.

Trumpism finds its main electoral support base primarily in the petite bourgeoisie, even while it mostly serves the interests of ruling class corporate and finance capital.

---

9   Nate Cohn, "Why Trump Won: Working-Class Whites," *New York Times*, November 9, 2016.

10 Anthony DiMaggio, "Election Con 2016: New Evidence Demolishes the Myth of Trump's 'Blue-Collar' Populism," *Counterpunch*, June 16, 2017, https://www.counterpunch.org/2017/06/16/93450/.

It is true that candidate Trump *posed* as a populist champion of America's forgotten heartland working class and a critic of the Wall Street elite. But Trump's backers were concerned primarily with the reactionary "social issues" that the orange plutocrat championed on behalf of the far right, not working-class economic grievances against the capitalist establishment. Sexism, nativism, and racism (white identity) were the leading correlates with Trump voting, not socio-economic dissatisfaction or disadvantage. It was Trump's chauvinistic positions and statements on race, gender and immigration—not his deceptive outward "blue-collar populism"—that scored him the most points with his mostly middle-class backers.

Nearly 60 percent of white people without college degrees who voted for Trump were in the top half of the income distribution.

Defined as Caucasians with less than a college degree, the "white working class" demonstrated its usual neoliberal-era preference for Republicans over Democrats in the presidential election. (Trump bested Clinton among white voters without college degrees by 66 percent to 28 percent, the biggest Republican margin with those voters since 1980.)[11] But the lack of a college diploma is a highly imperfect measure of working-class status. Bill Gates never got a bachelor's degree. Neither did his proletarian comrade Mark Zuckerberg. Occupation and income are far better indicators (exit polls include the second category but not the first). Nearly 60 percent of white people without college degrees who voted for Trump were in the top half of the income distribution.[12] One in five white Trump voters without a college degree had a household income over $100,000.

Another difficulty with the white Trumpenproletarian narrative is that most whites without an allegedly class-defining college degree don't vote. Thanks in part to this silent election boycott, Trump won with approximately just a fifth of the 136 million white American adults who lack the higher ed sheepskin.[13]

11 Gary Langer, et al, ABC News, "Huge Margin Among Working-Class Whites Lifts Trump to a Stunning Election Upset," November 9, 2016, https://abcnews.go.com/Politics/huge-margin-working-class-whites-lifts-trump-stunning/story?id=43411948.

12 Nicholas Carnes and Norm Lupu, "It's Time to Bust the Myth: Most Trump Voters were Not Working Class," *Washington Post*, June 5, 2017, https://www.washingtonpost.com/news/monkey-cage/wp/2017/06/05/its-time-to-bust-the-myth-most-trump-voters-were-not-working-class/.

13 Kim Moody, "Who Put Trump in the White House?" *Jacobin*, January 11, 2017, https://www.jacobinmag.com/2017/01/trump-election-democrats-gop-clinton-whites-workers-rust-belt/.

There was no mass white working class outpouring for Trump. Clinton's miserable, centrist campaign and Obama's neoliberal legacy depressed multi-racial and cross-ethnic working- and lower-class voter turnout, opening the door for Trump to squeak by.[14] Racist voter suppression in contested states helped.[15] *Slate* writers Konstantin Kilibarda and Daria Roithmayr got it right three weeks after the election: "*Donald Trump didn't flip working-class white voters,*" they wrote, "*Hillary Clinton lost them....* Relative to the 2012 election, Democratic support in the key Rust Belt states [Iowa, Michigan, Ohio, Pennsylvania, and Wisconsin] collapsed as *a huge number of Democrats stayed home* or (to a lesser extent) voted for a third party." The decline of working-class Democratic voters between 2012 and 2016 was much bigger than the rise of working-class Republican voters in the "Rust Belt Five." Among those earning less than $50,000 a year there, the decline in Democratic voting was 3.5 times greater than the rise in Republican voting. Among white voters in general, the decline in Democratic voting was 2.1 times greater than the growth in Republican voting.[16] The image of poor and working-class whites flocking to Trump was and remains a remarkably durable *myth*.

The most relevant factor behind Trump's success in winning over the majority of "white working-class" voters was the decision by so many in the working class not to vote, thanks to the neoliberal nothingness of the onetime purported "party of the people."[17] This is the truth behind Bernie Sanders's statement to the 2017 People's Summit in Chicago: "Trump didn't win the election. The Democratic Party lost the election."[18] It lost because the party has abandoned workers' lunch-pail economic issues and the language of class in pursuit of corporate sponsorship and votes from the professional class.[19]

The image of poor and working-class whites flocking to Trump was and remains a remarkably durable myth.

---

14 Paul Street, "'Progressive' Obama: He's Melting, He's Melting," *Counterpunch*, June 19, 2015, https://www.counterpunch.org/2015/06/19/progressive-obama-hes-melting-hes-melting/; Lance Selfa, ed., *U.S. Politics in an Age of Uncertainty* (Chicago: Haymarket Books, 2018).

15 Greg Palast,."The Election was Stolen—Here's How," *Greg Palast Investigative Journalism*, November 11, 2016, https://www.gregpalast.com/election-stolen-heres/.

16 Konstantin Kilibarda and Daria Roithmayr, "The Myth of the Rustbelt Revolt," *Slate*, December 1, 2016, https://slate.com/news-and-politics/2016/12/the-myth-of-the-rust-belt-revolt.html (emphasis added).

17 Lance Selfa, *The Democrats: A Critical History* (Chicago: Haymarket Books, 2012); Paul Street, *Barack Obama and the Future of American Politics* (New York: Routledge, 2008).

18 Bernie Sanders, "The Political Revolution Now," June 10, 2017, https://www.youtube.com/watch?v=6MknMeS5bGQ.

19 Thomas Frank, *What's the Matter with Kansas?* (New York: Picador, 2005); Thomas Frank, *Listen, Liberal: Whatever Happened to the Party of the People?* (New York: Picador, 2017).

A "Strong Leader" to Punish Liberal and Left Elites and Make Whites Supreme Again

What about Trump's barely hidden racism? This too is not a problem for Trump backers.

Many liberals have been stunned that Trump's clear corruption and taste for tyranny does not ever seem to bother his base. This liberal astonishment is naïve. In December 2015, political scientist Matthew MacWilliams surveyed 1,800 registered voters across the US and the political spectrum. Employing standard statistical survey analysis, MacWilliams found that education, income, gender, and age had no significant bearing on a Republican voter's presidential candidate preference. "Only two of the variables I looked at," MacWilliams reported in January of 2016, "were statistically significant: authoritarianism, followed by fear of terrorism, though *the former was far more significant than the latter.*" Trump was "the only candidate in either party with statistically significant support from authoritarians," MacWilliams found. "Those who say a Trump presidency 'can't happen here should check their conventional wisdom at the door.... *Conditions are ripe for an authoritarian leader to emerge. Trump is seizing the opportunity.*"[20]

A year and a half later, a poll conducted by political scientists Ariel Malka and Yphtach Lelkes found that 56 percent of Republicans chillingly supported postponing the 2020 presidential election if Trump and congressional Republicans advocated it, to "make sure that only eligible American citizens can vote."[21]

What about Trump's barely hidden racism, evident from his numerous statements before and during his presidency? This too is *not* a problem for Trump backers. Trump's disproportionately Caucasian base is fused by an embattled white racial identity.[22] The Trumpian "make America white again" (really, "make white men supreme again") heart- and mind-set holds that whites are becoming a minority targeted by discrimination, and "politically correct" liberals and leftists have

---

20 Matthew MacWilliams, "The One Weird Trait That Predicts Whether You're a Trump Supporter," *Politico Magazine* (January 2016), https://www.politico.com/magazine/story/2016/01/donald-trump-2016-authoritarian-213533 (emphasis added).
21 Ariel Malka and Yphtach Lelkes, "In a new poll, half of Republicans say they would support postponing the 2020 election if Trump proposed it," *Washington Post*, August 10, 2017, https://www.washingtonpost.com/news/monkey-cage/wp/2017/08/10/in-a-new-poll-half-of-republicans-say-they-would-support-postponing-the-2020-election-if-trump-proposed-it/.
22 Eric Draitser, "Donald Trump and the Triumph of White Identity Politics," *Counterpunch*, March 24, 2017, https://www.counterpunch.org/2017/03/24/donald-trump-and-the-triumph-of-white-identity-politics/.

been turning the nation's politics and policies against white values, culture, needs, rights, and prerogatives. This white victimhood perception of "reverse discrimination" (devoid of evidence for its claims) informs the Trump base's understanding of the meaning of the word "corruption" in ways the liberal writer Peter Beinart recently captured in *The Atlantic*. For Trump's base, Beinart wrote in the summer of 2018, the idea of corruption wasn't about money, politics, and the law. It was about racial and gender purity and hierarchy:

> Trump supporters appear largely unfazed by the mounting evidence that Trump is the least ethical president in modern American history.... Once you grasp that for Trump and many of his supporters, *corruption means less the violation of law than the violation of established hierarchies* [of race and gender], *their behavior makes more sense. ...* Why were Trump's supporters so convinced that [Hillary] Clinton was the more corrupt candidate even as reporters uncovered far more damning evidence about Trump's foundation than they did about Clinton's? Likely because Clinton's candidacy threatened traditional gender roles. For many Americans, female ambition—especially in service of a feminist agenda—in and of itself represents a form of corruption. When Trump's former personal attorney testified to Congress about Trump's longstanding personal and political corruption, it made it harder for Republicans to claim that Trump hadn't violated the law. But for many if not most Republicans, Trump remained uncorrupt—indeed, anti-corrupt—because what they *fear most isn't the corruption of American law; it's the corruption of America's traditional identity.* And in the struggle against *that form of corruption*— the kind embodied by Cristhian Rivera [the "illegal immigrant" accused of murdering the young white woman Mollie Tibbetts in rural Iowa two weeks ago]—*Trump isn't the problem. He's the solution.*[23]

Among Trump's base, white racial identity and authoritarianism are merged and cross-fertilized in the angry and muddled minds of the Trumpenvolk. In May 2018, in a paper titled "White Outgroup Intolerance and Declining Support for American Democracy," political scientists Steven V. Miller and Nicholas T. Davis found a strong correlation between white Americans' racial intolerance and their support for authoritarian rule. "When racially intolerant white people fear [that] democracy may benefit marginalized people of color," NBC News reported, citing Miller and Davis's paper, "they abandon their commitment to democracy." The Trump base's bigotry and its leanings toward authoritarianism, Miller and David determined, were inseparably linked. When Trump calls Mexicans murderers and rapists, when he rails about building a southern border wall, when he denounces the media as "fake news," when he dismisses jury verdicts

Political scientists Steven V. Miller and Nicholas T. Davis found a strong correlation between white Americans' racial intolerance and support for authoritarian rule.

---

23 Peter Beinart, "Why Trump Supporters Believe He is Not Corrupt," *The Atlantic*, August 22, 2018, https://www.theatlantic.com/ideas/archive/2018/08/what-trumps-supporters-think-of-corruption/568147/ (emphasis added).

and the rule of law, and insults judges based on their nationality, and when he praises authoritarian leaders, he is appealing to one, seamless block of voters.

The most sophisticated and statistically astute analysis of the 2016 Trump electorate produced was crafted by political sociologists David Norman Smith and Eric Hanley. In an article published in *Critical Sociology* in March 2018, Smith and Hanley found that Trump's white base was differentiated from white non-Trump voters not by class or other "demographic" factors (including income, age, gender, and the alleged class identifier of education) but by eight key attitudes and values: identification as "conservative;" support for "domineering leaders;" Christian fundamentalism; prejudice against immigrants; prejudice against Blacks; prejudice against Muslims; prejudice against women; and a sense of pessimism about the economy. Strong Trump supporters scored particularly high on support for domineering leaders, fundamentalism, opposition to immigrants, and economic pessimism. They were particularly prone to support authoritarian leaders who promised to respond punitively to minorities perceived as "line cutters"—"undeserving" others who were allegedly getting ahead of traditional white Americans in the procurement of jobs and government benefits—and to the supposed liberal "rotten apples" who were purportedly allowing these "line cutters" to advance ahead of traditional white American males.[24]

Since Trump's election there has been an anomalous spike in hate crimes concentrated in counties where Trump won by larger margins.

Support for politically authoritarian leaders and a sense of intolerance regarding racial, ethnic, and gender differences are two sides of the same Trumpian coin. The basic desire animating Trump's base was "the defiant wish for a domineering and impolitic leader" linked to "the wish for a reversal of what his base perceives as an inverted moral and racial order."

---

24 David Norman Smith and Eric Hanley, "The Anger Games: Who Voted for Trump and Why," *Critical Sociology* (March 2018), https://journals.sagepub.com/doi/abs/10.1177/0896920517740615.

Presidential Rhetoric and Hate Crimes

Here we are three years after Trump shocked contemporary Doremus Jessups by showing that yes, a neofascist president could happen here.[25] At its ugliest fringes, Trump's base has gone beyond mere electoral and rhetorical support for Trump's racist and nativist policies and engaged in lethal violence influenced by Trump's hateful and conspiratorial rhetoric. Indeed, Trump's fueling of intolerance and bigotry has had an ugly impact. A recent investigation by ABC News found twenty-nine criminal cases nationwide where perpetrators echoed "presidential" rhetoric. These included ten cases where the perpetrators either cheered or defended Trump while "taunting or threatening others," the network reported. "On another 10 occasions, defendants justified their violent or threatening behavior in court by citing the president and his rhetoric. In nine other cases, Trump was hailed by perpetrators either during or after physically attacking innocent victims."[26]

The Brookings Institution reports that "FBI data show that since Trump's election there has been an anomalous spike in hate crimes concentrated in counties where Trump won by larger margins. It was the second-largest uptick in hate crimes in the 25 years for which data are available, second only to the spike after September 11, 2001." Brookings referenced an Anti-Defamation League study showing that "counties that hosted a Trump campaign rally in 2016 saw hate crime rates more than double compared to similar counties that did not host a rally."

The deranged shooter who killed eleven Jewish Americans at the Tree of Life synagogue in November 2018 was inspired by Trump's right-wing anti-immigrant rhetoric (the synagogue was targeted not just because of its Judaism but also because of its commitment to helping immigrants settle in the US). Ditto the Texas killer who slaughtered twenty-two people at a "Mexican" Wal-Mart near the US–Mexico border in August 2019. The El Paso shooter's manifesto mirrored Trump's inflammatory rhetoric about a criminal Latinx "invasion" of the United States.[27]

The deranged shooter who killed eleven Jewish Americans at the Tree of Life synagogue was inspired by Trump's right-wing anti-immigrant rhetoric.

---

25 Doremus Jessup is the middle class liberal-left journalist protagonist in Sinclair Lewis's widely read 1935 novel *It Can't Happen Here*. Lewis depicted a fascist takeover of the United States. His leading character Jessup and numerous other liberals and progressives naively dismissed the possibility of fascist triumph in the "democratic" and constitutional-republican United States.

26 Mike Levine, "'No Blame?' ABC News finds 36 cases invoking 'Trump' in connection with violence, threats, alleged assaults." ABC News, August 14, 2019, https://abcnews.go.com/Politics/blame-abc-news-finds-17-cases-invoking-trump/story?id=58912889.

27 Guyette, "Is Trump a Fascist?"

Two Fascist Gatherings, December 2019

"Winning, Winning, Winning"

The conservative scholar Norman Ornstein warned that Trump might suspend the 2020 elections and declare martial law in order to stay in power.

At one of his regular fascist-style campaign rallies, on December 10, 2019, the very day that the US House rolled out Articles of Impeachment, Trump told an adoring Hershey, Pennsylvania, rally crowd that Senator Elizabeth Warren "has a fresh mouth."[28] The meaning of "fresh," certainly grasped by his audience, was that Warren was an impudent and uppity woman who talked back inappropriately to male superiors. Then Trump repeated his racist reference to Warren as "Pocohantas," a slight based on her claim of Native American ancestry.

Trump referred to FBI officials who dared to investigate his Russian connections as "scum" and denounced the "so-called articles of impeachment." He repeated his longstanding narrative about "illegal aliens" being murderers and rapists. He absurdly claimed that his poll numbers were "going through the roof." He preposterously called the centrist Democratic Party "the radical Left … party of socialism," claiming that the Democrats were trying to "overthrow the government" and supported a "socialized medicine" system that would take away Americans' right to choose their own doctors. He accused Democrats of wanting to "rip [infants] from their mothers' wombs" and "execute the baby!"

Trump boasted that the beloved right-wing racist president Ronald Reagan could never have attracted crowds the size of the ones who attend his rallies. The crowd roared when he invoked "Space Force"—a program for the increased militarization of space—and the recent US killing of two ISIS leaders, who he called "bloodthirsty savages."

While Trumpenvolk chanted "USA! USA!," Trump proclaimed that "America is Winning Again. America," Trump claimed, "is so respected"—a ludicrous claim in a world that is appalled by the Trump circus.

"The survival of our country is at stake. We will destroy our country if these people get in," Trump said in reference to Democrats running for president. "We are taking back our country," Trump said. "We are returning power to

---

28 View the rally in its revolting entirety here: https://www.youtube.com/watch?v=Ag11iGH1mZQ. Read a full transcript of the rally: https://www.rev.com/blog/donald-trump-hershey-pennsylvania-rally-transcript-december-10-2019.

the American people, to you." Trump thanked Pennsylvania and his backers for making the US "the greatest and most powerful country in the history of the world" and wrapped up with a classically fascist palingenetic-nationalist rant on America's greatness, "thriving," "unity," and triumph:

> With your help, and with your devotion, and your drive we are going to keep on working, we are going to keep on fighting, and we are going to keep on winning, winning, winning. We are going to keep on winning. We are one movement, one people, one family, and one glorious nation under God. America is thriving like never before. Ladies and gentlemen of Pennsylvania, the best is yet to come. Because together we will make America wealthy again, we will make America strong again, we will make America proud again, we will make America safe again, and we will make America great again.[29]

At one of many disturbing points in the rally, Trump said he might stay in office as long as another twenty-nine years. Just the previous Sunday, he had made a "joke" about remaining in office beyond his two-term constitutional limit, calling it "not a bad idea." Reflecting on that "joke" on the same day that Trump spoke in Hershey, the conservative American Enterprise Institute scholar Norman Ornstein tweeted that Trump would "do anything" to remain in office. He warned that Trump might suspend the 2020 elections and declare martial law in order to stay in power. Though seemingly far-fetched, such a possibility should not be considered "fanciful, alarmist or crazy," Ornstein said. The venerable Republican intellectual called on political and civic leaders, as well as law enforcement and military officials, to start "thinking now about how they might respond" if Trump attempts what would amount to a coup after the next election.[30]

When a woman protester was removed from the rally, the president screamed "Get her out" and then shamed the security guard expelling her for being too "politically correct" by removing the woman too gently, without violence. "Get her out. Get her out," Trump demanded while his supporters pointed and yelled at the demonstrator, who donned a #MeToo hat and held a sign that said: "Grabbing Power Back."

Angry Trump supporters interviewed after the Hershey rally told reporters that the removal of Trump would spark a "second Civil War." One old, white male

▼

Angry Trump supporters told reporters that the removal of Trump would spark a "second Civil War."

---

29 Ibid.
30 Norman Ornstein, @NormOrnstein, Twitter, December 10, 2019, https://twitter.com/NormOrnstein/status/1204481956169302019.

Trumpist said he'd respond to his hero's removal with his lethal weapon. "He is not going to be removed ... My .357 Magnum is comfortable with that. End of story," this menacing Trumpenvolk minion said. Another predicted an uprising by "seventy to eighty million Americans on the loose, not happy" (never mind that Trump got sixty million votes in 2016).[31]

"Please Never Stop Tweeting"

In interviews at a post-impeachment "Trumpstock" festival attended by a Republican Congressman and a Republican state representative in Golden Valley, Arizona, white Trumpists wearing red MAGA hats told *New York Times* reporter Astead Herndon of "a white America under threat as racial minorities typified by [Barack] Obama ... gain political power." The festival's attendees "described Trump as an inspirational figure who is undoing Mr. Obama's legacy [absurdly considered as radical and Left by Trumpists] and beating back the perceived threat of Muslim and Latino immigrants, whom they denounced in prejudiced terms." Trumpstock speakers linked Obama's middle name, Hussein, "to a false belief that he is a foreign-born Muslim." They described Democrats, in Herndon's words, as "not just political opponents, but of avatars of doom for Mr. Trump's predominantly white voter base and for the country."

"There is no difference between the democratic socialists [the Democratic Party] and the National Socialists," a "conservative" writer told Herndon, referring to Nazi Germany—an absurd case of the pot calling the kettle sooty. "Democrats," the writer said, "are the heirs to Adolf Hitler."

Trumpist singer Mona Fishman performed her songs "Fake News" and "Smells Like Soros." In one of her tunes, titled "Thank You Mr. President," she sang "please never stop tweeting. I can hardly wait to see what I'll be reading."

---

31 Tim Hains, "Trump Supporters In Hershey, PA Say There Would Be A 'Second Civil War' If Trump Is Removed From Office," *Real Clear Politics*, December 12, 2019, https:// www.realclearpolitics.com/video/2019/12/12/trump_supporters_in_hershey_pa_say_ there_would_be_a_second_civil_war_if_trump_is_removed_from_office.html

Another Trumpstocker, Mark Villatla, an older white man wearing a cowboy hat and a pistol, told Herndon that he'd been "stockpiling weapons, in case Mr. Trump's re-election is not successful."

"Nothing less than a civil war would happen," Mr Villatla said, his right hand reaching for a holstered handgun. "I don't believe in violence, but I'll do what I got to do."[32]

This is the stuff of fascism, happening here and now, in the United States of America.

Be Warned

How serious is the neofascist Trumpian threat to "American democracy," or what's left of it in the corporate-managed Huxwellian plutocracy that passes for popular self-government in the US?[33] We may get a good indication of how grave the danger is if the so-called opposition Democrats manage to overcome numerous hurdles—including their own cringing captivity to the nation's unelected and interrelated dictatorships of money and empire—to squeak out an Electoral College victory in November 2020. As Trump's former personal lawyer and "fixer" Michael Cohen, conservative scholar Norman Ornstein, and the still undercover White House official Anonymous tell us, Trump will likely cry foul, refuse to leave, and urge his "tough guy" backers within and beyond the nation's armed and police forces to resist the "radical Left" Democrats' "coup."[34]

How will Donito Trumpolini's fan-base followers respond? Nobody knows, of course, but we should take heed: the Trumpenvolk will not cotton to "democratic socialists" daring to remove their Great Tangerine God through the electoral process. Never mind that the compliant faux-opposition party of milquetoast

The Trumpenvolk will not cotton to "democratic socialists" daring to remove their Great Tangerine God through the electoral process.

---

32 Astead W. Herndon, *'Nothing Less Than a Civil War': These White Voters on the Far Right See Doom Without Trump,"* New York Times, December 28, 2019, https://www.nytimes.com/2019/12/28/us/politics/trump-2020-trumpstock.html.

33 Paul Street, *They Rule: The 1% v. Democracy* (New York: Routledge, 2014).

34 Kevin Breuninger and Dan Mangan, "Michael Cohen: 'I fear' Trump won't peacefully give up the White House if he loses the 2020 election," CNBC, February 27, 2019, https://www.cnbc.com/2019/02/27/michael-cohen-i-fear-trump-wont-give-up-the-white-house-if-he-loses-in-2020.html. Anonymous, *A Warning*, 242–43.

resistance, the Democrats, has rallied behind the center-right imperial corporatist Joe Biden. Distinctions between progressive-populists like Bernie Sanders and Alexandria Cortez, and neoliberal Democrats like Biden, are, like every other political and ideological distinction that matters, lost on Dear Leader Donald's base. The Trumpenvolk are impervious to rational persuasion. And this is the point: You don't reason with fascists. You organize against them and defeat them—and their sponsors and enablers, including the centrist Democrats who have demobilized and depressed the nation's progressive majority in neoliberal fealty to the wealthy few. ◀

The Trumpenvolk are impervious to rational persuasion. And this is the point: You don't reason with fascists.

The Vanguard of the White Revolution and Its Fertile Ground in Oregon

► **Shane Burley**

In 2011, I caught wind that a new fascist party had emerged in the United States. It was called the American Third Position Party (A3P) and had its origins in the anti-capitalist tradition of fascist politics that opposes both the cosmopolitanism of capitalism and the social equality of communism. They were running a former film director known for television Westerns named Merlin Miller, so I plugged his name in to see if there was any coverage on his campaign to get on the ballot.

What came up was a totally unknown podcast called *Vanguard Radio*, which labeled itself as "radical Traditionalist," a term popularized by fascist mystics like Julius Evola. Early in the interview it was clear that Miller was simply ignorant about American politics. He didn't even know what third position meant, and there was a tone shift when his interviewer realized he had to wear kid gloves

They believed that fixed identities (such as race and gender) drive who we are, and they believed who we are is fundamentally unequal.

with his subject. So my attention turned from Miller's nonsensical answers to the interviewer, whose voice was deep, measured in tone, with enthusiastic inflection, all of which suggested, to me anyway, an Ivy League education. By turns cordial and charming, the host's occasional, casual use of far-right jargon hinted there was something more under the surface, even if today he was going to let Miller rant uninterrupted in a facile way about patriotism.

I started going through other episodes of *Vanguard Radio*, and checking its website, AlternativeRight.com. Back then no one knew, or cared, who Richard Spencer was, but I had a sinking feeling in my stomach. He was good looking, he knew what he was talking about, and he was a dissident from inside the conservative movement. Spencer had already been radicalized by white nationalist politics even before he took a position at the *American Conservative* as an arts editor in 2007, but he steadily moved to the right as he encountered a new scene that was on the edges of the beltway politics of the right. This was the earliest days of the Alt Right (it was then still the "Alternative Right"), and Spencer was creating a space for the different brands of "dissident" far-rightists he was encountering: Paleoconservatives who had been kicked out of the GOP for their racialism, anti-immigration extremists, "folkish" racial pagans, fascist critics of free markets. There were a lot of these types who blended political ideas associated with both the left and the right, yet broke with the consensus of enlightenment politics in several key areas: they believed that fixed identities (such as race and gender) drive who we are, and they believed who we are is fundamentally unequal.[1] When Spencer was asked to define the Alternative Right and its founding principles, he said it was that people were "created unequal," a refrain he commonly used in speeches before he crystallized and popularized his later message about race and identity.[2]

I watched as Spencer built his brand, and he did it by hammering together earlier ideological trends. Many of his early converts—usually former staffers, writers, and academics who had become *persona non grata* in the conservative movement—came from paleoconservatism. This was a trend that had formed on

---

1 Shane Burley, *Fascism Today: What It Is and How to End It* (Chico, CA: AK Press, 2017), 59–62.
2 Richard Spencer, "The American Right: Can Americans Be Conservatives?" (speech to Traditional Britain Group, London, England, October 20th, 2012), https://www.youtube.com/watch?v=DSSKSK1ZHdI.

the fringes of the Republican Party that rejected the interventionalist "globalism" of the neoconservatives in favor of "Old Right" isolationism, extreme social conservatism, and the maintenance of antiquated social castes.[3] Old school white nationalism of the 1990s was a part of this new coalition, particularly the revived race science associated with figures like Steve Sailer and Jared Taylor and the *American Renaissance* newsletter. They had even taken on an effort to rebrand "race realism" a step further, now calling it "Human Biological Diversity" and presenting pseudo-scientific arguments for race and IQ and eugenics in the new language of science blogs.[4] Antisemitism was given new legs with the theories of evolutionary biologist Kevin MacDonald, now an editor of the white nationalist *Occidental Observer* run by a growing board of far-right celebrities like James Edwards and Sam Dickson, and funded, in part, by conservative publishing heir William Regnery. MacDonald argued that Judaism was a "group evolutionary strategy" Jews created to out-compete non-Jews for resources so they could wield tribal supremacy, and opined that ideologies of dissension (said to be primarily promulgated by Jews) were created specifically to disorganize gentiles into ignoring their natural nationalist impulses toward racial self-preservation. MacDonald's work had the effect of uniting anti-Semites behind a single semi-coherent theory and created a series of talking points about "Jewish Power" and the "Jewish Question" that would fuel their new ideological mission.[5]

The European New Right (ENR) may have been the biggest influence on this movement, which was a philosophic tradition amongst some far-right French academics to rebrand fascism using the language of "ethnopluralism," the creation of "anti-imperialist" autonomous communities to preserve racial tribalism.[6] It's on the esoteric side. Racialized heathenry, the pagan religion of Nordic peoples, played a heavy role, as did the Aryan spirituality of the traditionalist figures like Evola, who saw the world entering a dismal period of decline known as the "Kali Yuga," during which racial degeneracy runs rampant and the proper social

Evola, sitting to the political right of traditional fascism, wanted to return the world to what he saw as the original "Golden Age," when spiritual and racial elites ruled over their subordinates.

3   George Hawley, *Right-Wing Critics of American Conservatism* (Lawrence, University Press of Kansas, 2017), 178–200.
4   Burley, *Fascism Today*, 69–75.
5   Joan Braune, "Who's Afraid of the Frankfurt School? 'Cultural Marxism' as an Antisemitic Conspiracy Theory," *Journal for Social Justice* (2020): 6–9.
6   Jean-Yves Camus, "Alain de Benoist and the New Right," in *Key Thinkers of the Radical Right: Behind the New Threat to Liberal Democracy*, ed. Mark Sedgwick (New York: Oxford University Press, 2019), 73–86.

▼

There was a convergence taking place, and Alt Right messages about immigration, patriarchy, and "political correctness" were trending.

stratifications collapse. Evola, whom many cite as sitting to the political right of traditional fascism, wanted to return the world to what he saw as the original "Golden Age," when spiritual and racial elites ruled over their subordinates and spiritual traditions and hierarchies determined the course of societies. To effectualize that return, what was needed was a radical attack on modernity.[7] Organizations like the Asatru Folk Assembly, though marginal in numbers, helped sow some of the esoteric thinking that backed the concepts of the Alt Right, in particular "meta-genetics" and the "folkish" idea that Northern European pagan gods are the archetypes of this heritage. Much of this was not believed literally but was a return to a metaphorical and idealistic way of thinking, using myth and story to revitalize a glorious identity. This was part of what mobilized the Alt Right, the idea that they could intervene in history and "restart the world."

Externally, immigration was the issue on which they could recruit, by concentrating the focus of former influential Republicans like John Derbyshire and *VDare* founder Peter Brimelow. By framing the struggle for white survival as a universal historical concept they could present non-white immigration as an erosion of white society and an existential threat. This took a policy issue and made it a deeply paranoid emotional one, transforming their obsessive fascist worldview into one that employed the language of party politics.

This was a percolating movement, attracting waves of new recruits. Spencer used podcasting, which was still relatively novel, to draw in adherents, with interviews of movement figures, from Jared Taylor to conservative name-brands like Pat Buchanan. This was a space for conversion, for political development, for launching listeners on a journey into an above-ground, fascist, meta-political movement. It was a space to build identity.

And while the new Alternative Right had conferences and a lively publishing scene, it wasn't until 2015 that it really saw what was possible. The Alt Right began to merge, to some degree, with the online world of trolling found on web boards like 4Chan and /pol/, in particular bonding with the misogynist Men's Rights movement and the anti-democratic Neoreaction movement, popular in Silicon Valley. It was a meme'd movement, using irony and the punch of

---

7 Nicholas Goodrick-Clarke, *Black Sun: Aryan Cults, Esoteric Nazism, and the Politics of Identity* (New York City: NYU Press, 2003), 52–70.

young energy to push at the "politically correct" areas of neoliberalism.[8] There was a convergence taking place, and Alt Right messages about immigration, patriarchy, and "political correctness" were trending. A troll army had formed to attack the left, women, Jewish people, and people of color, using the pent-up rage and anonymity in places like 4Chan's /pol/board, where the only way you gained more respect was by outdoing your fellow troll's extremist rhetoric.

Then Trump said rapists were flooding across the border. This was when I knew that Richard Spencer had arrived.

In speech after speech, Spencer would say "something is happening," and it was. Alt Right conferences swelled, podcasts and publications emerged, and the rhetoric got more radical. "With a lot of these young kids they haven't read the book. They've watched a YouTube video that's given it all to them," said Spencer about the second generation of the Alt Right that was radicalizing online and flooding into his movement in advance of the 2017 Unite the Right rally. "And I don't say that to dismiss them because it's almost like some of us were smoking weed for years and tried a little cocaine, and some of these young kids injected heroin into their eyeball. They have come to these ideas much more quickly and in a much more intense fashion."[9] The movement accelerated and wanted to follow the example of the identitarian movement in Europe, Generation Identity in particular, and move from the world of online chatter and content production to action. This move was clunky at best, drawing from the ranks of student organizing that started in the earliest parts of the Trump campaign and coalescing into groups like Identity Evropa who were fighting against Muslim inclusion in their societies.[10] The larger movement tried on different ways of organizing, but never got the right fit, alternating between microscopic flashmob-styled rallies and private events that were getting shut down one after another. There was a contradiction here, between their public and their private rhetoric, between their vision of the future and their inability to realize it because of their desperate lack of organizing skills.[11]

The movement accelerated and wanted to follow the example of the identitarian movement in Europe.

8   George Hawley, *Making Sense of the Alt-Right* (New York: Columbia University Press, 2017), 67–90.
9   *Alt-Right: Days of Rage*. Directed by Adam Bhala Lough. Los Angeles: Alldayeveryday, 2018.
10 Author Interview with Nathan Damigo, May 24, 2017.
11 Shane Burley, "Alt Right 2.0," *Salvage*, July 6, 2017, https://salvage.zone/online-exclusive/alt-right-2-0/.

Oregon was founded as a white utopia in which Black people were formally banned from residence (on threat of corporal punishment).

The Alt Right was not the originator of what was becoming a global far-right surge, but now it was emergent all across the US as Trump gave voice to its angst. Rural areas, which have been wedded to the GOP since the shift toward cultural conservatism in the 1980s, were attracted to the national populist message offered by the Trumpian right. The militias that crystalized in these regions relied on a Christian "constitutionalist" ideological reconstruction and mobilized class resentments, not against their employers, bosses, or the political and corporate class but against the marginalized members of their communities. The anger was directed horizontally: at environmentalists, say, or at communities of color, public employees, the urban poor, and many others cast in the light of the enemy other. A narrative developed among disaffected segments of the rural base, setting "producers" (of food, raw materials, and manufactured goods) against the "parasite" class. The "producers" turned against the federal government, which they viewed as enabler and protector of the undesirables and the social ills that accompany them.[12] As manufacturing jobs disappeared, unions were crushed, large agribusiness attacked small farming, and social safety net programs vanished from rural counties, a culture of desperation arose. Without the left to mobilize them along economic issues, rural America turned to right populism to fill that void, and Trump helped push them further to the right. The Patriot militias, which were anti-government right-wing formations founded on conspiracy theories, stood in seeming heroic fashion to bridge the gaps in community support, often performing services like medical transport that were difficult to find in these areas.[13]

This perfect storm of white rage, ranging from the Alt Right to the militia movement, hit Oregon hard, but only because the state was already primed for it. Oregon's history is often misconstrued as one of simple good-natured liberal gentrification. In fact, Oregon was founded as a white utopia in which Black people were formally banned from residence (on threat of corporal punishment), and consecrated amid racist expulsions of Chinese and Japanese residents. This was a state where white labor rights were won only with the total erasure of non-white workers. Oregon was where the Ku Klux Klan in the 1920s flowered in its second era (during those years, the KKK had upwards of four million

---

12 Chip Berlet and Spencer Sunshine, "Rural rage: the roots of right-wing populism in the United States," *The Journal of Peasant Studies* 46, issue 3 (2019): 480–513.

13 Shane Burley, "Google Jewish Bankers," *Journal for Social Justice* (2020): 4–12.

70   Unflattering Photos of Fascists

members in the US), hosting its second largest constituency (behind Indiana), and where the Klan dominated local Democratic politics from 1922–25. These foundations would make Oregon central to the later development of the white power movement, from Aryan Nations to neo-nazi skinheads, and the far-right base metastasizing in cities today.

Right-wing Oregonians—of which there are still many, despite the state's granola-left image—have always hated the cities, even from within them. And so the Alt Right and the Trump campaign provided an anchor point from which to fight back. The characterization of Oregon as a firm Blue State that could never be swayed far to the right misses an understanding of the formula that makes a fascist movement: working class white anger is the tinder, nationalism is the match.

Working class white anger is the tinder, nationalism is the match.

Once the community was primed for the fight, the Alt Right and other white nationalists were ready to dive in. "Independent Trumpists"—the enthusiastic base of supporters, personalities, and organizations who, while not formally associated with Trump or the GOP, have become his foot soldiers—began to show up.[14] In Oregon, this was led primarily by Patriot Prayer, an organization built around the personality of its founder, Joey Gibson, and his acolytes. They were there to attract a big tent of supporters, and they did, including everyone from Patriot groups to the Alt-Light street-gang the Proud Boys to open white nationalist organizations like the National Socialist Movement, the Daily Stormer Book Club, and Identity Evropa. The militias were already agitated, first occupying the Sugar Pine Mine in Southern Oregon in 2015 before riding the wave of Bunkerville to the forty-one-day occupation of the Malheur Wildlife Refuge in Harney County. Grazing, land, mineral, and logging rights were all on the table, and with Trump pitting environmentalists (a rhetorical proxy for urban liberals) against economically vulnerable Patriots (proxy for "producers"), he was able to push the militias to action.

Patriot Prayer ran on this energy through the election, holding a sequence of high-profile rallies that brought out an antifascist opposition because of Gibson's unwillingness to expel the racist element. After a Patriot Prayer attendee, Jeremy Christian, murdered two people on a Portland train during a racist attack,

---

14 Spencer Sunshine, "The Growing Alliance Between Neo-Nazis, Right Wing Paramilitaries and Trumpist Republicans," *Colorlines*, June 9, 2017, www.colorlines.com/articles/growing-alliance-between-neo-nazis-right-wing-paramilitaries-and-trumpist-republicans.

*Anti-fascist orga-
nizers escalated
their work. Alt
Right figures were
doxxed, fired, and
deplatformed, and
the movement's
main leaders
went into
retreat.*

tensions flared as rallies provided an opportunity for Patriot Prayer and the Proud Boys to stage violent assaults on counter-demonstrators. In the years that followed the election, the city ran on a schedule punctuated by beatings and street fights, where far-right groups trumpeted the threat of antifascists while disguising their own responsibility in politically motivated violence.[15] The Proud Boys escalated to totally unprovoked street attacks against people who dared to look askance at their instigations. These included queerphobic assaults that left the LGBTQ+ community quavering and created a sense that a red tide was rising, violence was all around, choking people's neighborhoods as it asserted itself.

Was it just the Proud Boys, or was it an entire slice of the state? How far would the violence go?

The rest of the country followed a similar pattern, seeing an increased Alt Right presence both inside and outside of Washington. Outlets like *Breitbart* and *Rebel Media* started to echo white nationalist talking points, and Trump's election ushered in figures connected to white nationalism as advisors and policymakers. Stephen Miller, a former college friend of Richard Spencer, set his sites on immigrants, using his position as a senior policy advisor to launder the noxious ideas normally found in *VDare*.[16]

The Alt Right was at a point of ascendency. Then the August 2017 Unite the Right rally in Charlottesville dealt them a major setback amid a botched march and the murder of protestor Heather Heyer. Anti-fascist organizers escalated their work. Alt Right figures were doxxed, fired, and deplatformed, and the movement's main leaders went into retreat.

Richard Spencer withdrew from the spotlight, no longer the fashionable leader he had hoped to be. But he had made his permanent mark on the world.[17] In Portland and across the country, he had made the most extreme forms of white identitarianism and xenophobia seem mundane. The Alt Right pushed the

---

15 Shane Burley, "How Patriot Prayer Is Building a Violent Far-Right Movement in Portland," *Truthout*, June 19, 2018, truthout.org/articles/how-patriot-prayer-is-building-a-violent-far-right-movement-in-portland.

16 Michael Edison Hayden, "Stephen Miller's Affinity for White Nationalism Revealed in Leaked Emails," *Hatewatch*, November 12, 2019, splcenter.org/hatewatch/2019/11/12/stephen-millers-affinity-white-nationalism-revealed-leaked-emails.

17 Shane Burley, "The Autumn of the Alt Right," *Commune*, https://communemag.com/the-autumn-of-the-alt-right/.

Overton window of acceptable political discourse further to the right on race.[18] The bad look for the Alt Right in no way presages a decline of white nationalism. On the contrary, Trump's rise has fortified their foundations. With increased social instability, anything is possible. White identity politics has gone from *sub rosa* to popularly branded, and white nationalism is now part of the spectrum of normal American political expression.

"Tolerant Oregon" is no exception to this shift, and in a way was the vanguard, showing the cracks in community and the failure of liberal urban politics to repel virulent racism and xenophobia. There are peaks and troughs, and leaders emerge and fade away, but what Spencer built is still here. ◄

18 Derek Robertson, "How an Obscure Conservative Theory Became the Trump Era's Go-to Nerd Phrase," *Politico*, February 25, 2018, politico.com/magazine/story/2018/02/25/overton-window-explained-definition-meaning-217010.

From Portlandia to Portlantifa:

Notes on the Development of a Movement

▶ **Tizz Bee**

In November 2016, Portland was rocked by a week of militant street demonstrations after the election of Donald Trump. The height of the activity occurred on November 10, when tens of thousands hit the streets to express their rage. A march organized by Portland's Resistance—an organization led by members from various groups in the local movement for Black lives—eventually intersected with a contingent of Black youth and local anarchists who had gathered outside of Holladay Park. After a few speeches, the march continued and began to take on an atmosphere of joyous rebellion. "Fuck Donald Trump," by YG, became the theme song of the evening as youth smashed city infrastructure and private property and set dumpsters alight. When the smoke cleared, over one million dollars of damage had been done in the Pearl District, and in subsequent days several more rounds of rioting followed before the flames were quelled.

The riots of 2016 widened the Overton window of the street tactics that local movements would use to resist the rise of the reactionary far-right in the coming years. As local grassroots movements continue to struggle against institutionalized racism, against organized white supremacist gangs, and against a growing local militia movement, this has set the stage for the transformation of complacent bourgeois Portlandia to what some call Portlantifa.

Roots of the Movement

From its founding in 1844 and until 1954, Oregon's Black exclusion laws made it illegal for Black people to move to the state. If they dared to come, they faced the threat of lashings, economic sanction, and deportation. In the early half of the twentieth century Oregon was known as the most racist state north of the Mason-Dixon line. In the 1920s, both Portland's mayor and the governor of Oregon were open KKK members, and the city's famous Rose Parade would routinely culminate in cross burnings on top of the local lookout at Mt. Tabor. Until the rise of the civil rights movement, Portland was as segregated as any city in the South, with racist real estate laws—known as "redlining"—that banned the sale of homes to black residents outside of certain neighborhoods in North Portland.[1]

The civil rights movement of the 1950s evolved into the militant struggle for Black liberation in the 1960s and 70s alongside a growing anti-war movement. In response to heavy-handed, racist police tactics, Portland saw major rioting for two days in the summer of 1967 and then again in 1968.[2] Hundreds of thousands of dollars in damage occurred, and militant Black youth called for the autonomy of the historically Black Albina neighborhood.[3] The creation of the Portland Black Panther party by founder Kent Ford in 1969 marked the beginning of serious organizing efforts against the city's discriminatory housing and urban development policy, establishing mutual aid programs and opposing police brutality.[4] The work

Portland has never stopped being a battleground between violent racism and those who seek to defend communities.

---

1   Karen J. Gibson, "Bleeding Albina: A History of Community Disinvestment, 1940–2000," *Transforming Anthropology* 15, no. 1 (2007): 3–25.
2   Ayodale Braimah, "Albina Riot, Portland, Oregon (1967)," *Black Past*, November 26, 2017.
3   Oregon Historical Society. 16mm Portland (OR) Civil Rights KOIN News Pull - MI# 07523 (R1). YouTube. https://www.youtube.com/watch?v=vM9NIovE1i0.
4   Lucas N. N. Burke and Judson L. Jeffries, *The Portland Black Panthers: Empowering Albina and Remaking a City* (Seattle: University of Washington Press, 2016).

of the Panthers was instrumental in kickstarting Portland's "neighborhood revolution," which sought community control over urban development processes and produced, for a time, a more radical version of today's neighborhood association system. In Portland, as in other places, these social movements began pushing back and winning against racism, war, and ecological destruction.

Portland's vibrant antifascist movement grew from the backbone of seasoned antifascist organizing and the decades of street fighting that came with it.

Swing of the Pendulum

The wave of relative progress in the 1960s and 70s was followed by a vicious countercurrent of reaction in the 1980s. Partially spurred on by the racist rhetoric of the Reagan administration and its "Southern Strategy," far-right racist groups were emboldened to take more violent action across the country. Groups like White Aryan Resistance (WAR), led by the notorious Tom Metzger, promoted white supremacist violence and inspired a movement of racist skinhead gangs, such as East Side White Pride, whose members, in 1988, murdered Portland resident and Ethiopian immigrant Mulugeta Seraw.[5] The eventual rise of Volksfront and the street-prison gang European Kindred extended the campaign of racist street attacks in the city through the mid-1980s and early 1990s, which continue to this day.

As a result of the violence, militant groups with capable street fighters began organizing to resist the assaults. Anti-Racist Action held its first national gathering in Portland during the Tom Metzger trial in 1991 to oppose a rally in his support.[6] Soon after, racist groups also began to take casualties. In 1993 racist skinhead Eric Banks was shot dead by John Bair, a member of Skin Heads Against Racial Prejudice.[7]

Portland has never stopped being a battleground between violent racism and those who seek to defend communities. In 2017, in what become known as the Max Station Stabbing, two of three people, Taliesin Myrddin Namkai-Meche

---

5 Elinor Langer, *A Hundred Little Hitlers: The Death of a Black Man, the Trial of a White Racist, and the Rise of the Neo-Nazi Movement in America* (New York: Metropolitan Books, 2003).

6 Anti-Racist Action, https://antiracistaction.org/history/.

7 Jason Wilson, "Portland's Dark History of White Supremacy," *The Guardian*, May 31, 2017, www.theguardian.com/us-news/2017/may/31/portland-white-supremacy-racism-train-stabbing-murder.

and Ricky John Best, lost their lives defending two teenage girls against the attacks of murderous white supremacist Jeremy Christian, leaving only survivor Micah Fletcher to tell the tale of the latest installment in a long story of violence. In 2016, two members of European Kindred ran over and killed Larnel Bruce, a Black teenager, and in 2010, a white supremacist shot and paralyzed anti-racist skinhead Luke V. Querner. The veterans of these struggles against organized white supremacist gangs have played a huge rule in developing a rejuvenated antifascist culture in Portland.

Cops and Klan Go Hand and Hand

Portland's vibrant antifascist movement grew from the backbone of seasoned antifascist organizing and the decades of street fighting that came with it. The current iteration of Portland's antifascist movement arose from a lineage of intergenerational militant struggle. This struggle has cost many people their lives, and others long terms of imprisonment. The movement gained its youthful rigor, mass street-mobilizing capacity, and tear-gas endurance from those who earned experience in the 2010s from consistent street confrontations with the police during the movement for Black lives and in response to the systematic murder of members of Portland's Black community by the Portland Police Bureau.

In 2010, Portland witnessed a return to militant black bloc anarchist tactics in the wake of a series of murders by police that included the slaying of Aaron Campbell and Keaton Otis. Members of the black community and Portland's anarchist scene began organizing together, such as in the campaign to get killer cop Ronald Frashour fired. After the rapid rise and fall of Occupy Portland, the local movements for black lives quickly followed, and they continued to welcome anarchist participation and solidarity in years of oppositional street demonstrations. The development of these intersectional relationships forged the foundations of today's antifascist movement in the city.

After the 2016 riots, 2017 was a year of almost monthly militant demonstrations and counterdemonstrations against ultra-nationalist groups—a trend that has continued and only mildly decreased in recent years. It was during these early months that local antifascist Sean D. Kealiher began speaking to thousands at demonstrations before he was martyred. Sean worked to expand what

2017 was a year of almost monthly militant demonstrations and counterdemonstrations against ultra-nationalist groups.

"resistance" meant and introduced thousands of activists to militant antifascism by pushing back against liberal reformist pacifism in words and actions, profoundly altering the political culture of grassroots movements in the city.

We remember all those who have lost their lives in recent years, including David John Busby, aka Phoenix; Sean D. Kealiher; Taliesin Myrddin Namkai-Meche; and Ricky John Best. We refuse to forget those who are still behind bars, including Damion Feller, Gage Halupowski, and William Pierce.

Oregon, like many states, is riven by deep political divisions between its urban and rural communities, under-laid by economic realities.

Extractive Industry, Ranchers and Suburban Patriots

Portland's antifascist struggle rages in a state where the social and economic stratifications of an extractive capitalistic system not only threatened us with growing authoritarianism but are leading us to the brink of ecological collapse. Oregon, like many states, is riven by deep political divisions between its urban and rural communities, underlaid by economic realities. As urban centers like Portland become "creative hubs" for the new precarious gig economy dominated by corporations like Uber and Amazon, rural areas are still lorded over by timber and mining conglomerates, and local cattle-ranching barons.

As urban populations grow, they gain influence in state legislatures. In Oregon, environmental and climate protection bills have become a lightning rod of conflict. The new violent right-wing in the state is marked by a growing radical anti-government militia movement and suburban patriot groups dedicated to "cleansing the streets." All of these groups have affinities for or actual ties to extractive industries, cattle ranching barons, and the Trump administration.

The armed occupation of the Malheur National Wildlife Refuge by right-wing followers of Ammon Bundy and his militiamen is an example of increasingly aggressive rural bourgeoisie bent on grabbing land. The primary goal of the occupation, according to Bundy, was the release of ranchers Dwight and Steven Hammond who had been charged criminally with burning protected public lands and, prior to their arsons, had illegally grazed cattle on the commons. Additionally, Bundy sought to force the federal government to relinquish control of public land to "get the economics here in the county revived" primarily for logging and grazing.[8] It ended with a jury finding the Bundys not guilty on all charges related to the occupation, and Trump pardoning the Hammonds.[9]

Longtime Oregon lumber baron Andrew Miller, owner of Stimson Lumber, is known to support a plethora of far-right campaigns across the state through the Oregon Transformation Project PAC. Recently, Stimson Lumber moved thousands of jobs out of state to put pressure on state officials to abate and rescind climate-related legislation.[10] Miller is also a strong supporter of the "Timber Unity" campaign's rallies in support of Republican walkouts in the state legislature over opposition to a cap and trade bill in 2019.[11] An anti-government militia group known as the Three Percenters backed the walkout by flaunting arms in support of the Republican state senators, amid threats of arrest by the governor, before they fled the state and went into hiding.[12] After several days of consecutive days of demonstrations, including by armed Three Percenters and logging trucks ominously circling the state capital, the Timber Unity campaign received an official invitation by Donald Trump to take a "victory lap" in a visit to the White House.[13]

Three Percenter groups have also been invited to take on an official security role by James Buchal, the chair of the Multnomah County Republicans.[14] (Portland

Patriot Prayer formed in the fires of the 2016 post-Trump election riots.

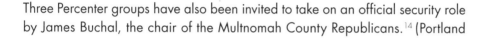

8   CBS News/Associated Press, "Oregon militia in standoff with feds names themselves," January 4, 2016, https://www.cbsnews.com/news/oregon-militia-names-themselves-citizens-for-constitutional-freedom/.
9   Eileen Sullivan and Julie Turkewitz, "Trump Pardons Oregon Ranchers Whose Case Inspired Wildlife Refuge Takeover," *The New York Times*, July 10, 2018, www.nytimes.com/2018/07/10/us/politics/trump-pardon-hammond-oregon.html.
10 Aaron Mesh. "Stimson Lumber Announces It's Pulling Timber Jobs Out of Oregon, in Rebuke to New Taxes and Carbon Caps," *Willamette Week*, May 31, 2019, https://www.wweek.com/news/2019/05/31/stimson-lumber-announces-its-pulling-timber-jobs-out-of-oregon-in-rebuke-to-new-taxes-and-carbon-caps/.
11 Nigel Jaquiss, "Truckers and Loggers Started a Rebellion in Oregon. Political Insiders Took It Over," Willamette Week, August 7, 2019, https://www.wweek.com/news/state/2019/08/07/truckers-and-loggers-started-a-rebellion-in-oregon-political-insiders-took-it-over/.
12 Nicole Javorsky, "Armed Extremists Just Escalated Oregon's Fight over Climate Legislation," *Mother Jones*, June 21, 2019, www.motherjones.com/politics/2019/06/armed-extremists-just-escalated-oregons-fight-over-climate-legislation/.
13 Aubrey Wieber and Claire Withycombe, "President Invites Timber Unity to Take D.C. Victory Lap." *Portland Tribune*, pamplinmedia.com/pt/432810-342186-president-invites-timber-unity-to-take-dc-victory-lap-.
14 Jason Wilson, "Portland Republicans to Use Militia for Security as Far-Right Rallies Continue," *The Guardian*, July 1, 2017, www.theguardian.com/us-news/2017/jul/01/portland-far-right-rally-republicans-militia-security.

sits in Multnomah County.) Buchal, an attorney, is a self-described libertarian who has built a career representing large industry interests in rural areas and combating environmental regulations.[15] Buchal and the Multnomah County Republicans were at the center of the Parade of Roses controversy that resulted in the right-wing group Patriot Prayer's first event in Portland on April 29, 2017, titled the "March for Free Speech."[16] Among the attendees was Jeremy Christian, who just a few months later was charged with murdering two people in the name of the same cause. Buchal is also the attorney for the right-wing agitator Joey Gibson, founder of Patriot Prayer. Patriot Prayer formed in the fires of the 2016 post-Trump election riots. Gibson is currently facing charges in the May Day 2019 attacks that he led against leftists at the Cider Riot Bar, which left multiple people severely injured.

Gibson is now the primary protagonist of right-wing incursions into Portland. Animated by a Christian ultra-nationalist worldview and armed with the rhetoric of restoring order to a city allegedly overrun by rioting, Gibson soon forged alliances with Three Percenter and Alt Right groups across the country. His June 4, 2017 rally saw hundreds of members of the Alt Right converge on Portland from across the country, including Kyle "Based Stickman" Chapman and John Turano, a.k.a. "Based Spartan," both of whom built reputations as violent street fighters while donning pro-wrestling costumes and personas. At the same rally, the Three Percenters were discovered assisting Department of Homeland Security agents in making "citizen arrests" of protesters. Three Percenters were also found to have set up sniper positions on rooftops at an August 4, 2018 rally—which Portland Police knew at the time but did not divulge until months later.

Police collaboration with Patriot Prayer is extremely alarming. It is a harbinger of the quiet support among police for Gibson's violent right-wing political praxis. In August 2018, police were seen shooting flash bangs directly at antifascist protesters while ensconced among Patriot Prayer goons. The flash bang assault caused a serious head injury to one person, whose life was saved because he was wearing a helmet. Then Police Chief Danielle Outlaw made clear which side she was on by appearing on local right-wing radio host Lars Larson's

> *Three Percenters were also found to have set up sniper positions on rooftops at an August 4, 2018 rally—which Portland Police knew at the time.*

---

15 James L. Buchal, Complex Civil Litigation Specialist, www.buchal.com/legal.htm.

16 FOX 12 Staff, "Annual 82nd Avenue of Roses Parade Cancelled Due to 'Threats of Violence,'" *KPTV.com*, 30 Aug. 2018, www.kptv.com/news/annual-nd-avenue-of-roses-parade-canceled-due-to-threats/article_f8247525-42ba-5a56-a38c-042fffb9be5a.html.

show and characterizing public outcry over the police brutality as "protesters who were acting like children who lost a schoolyard fight and had gone off to whine and complain."[17] Later, it was learned that Patriot Prayer had long been coordinating with Portland Police Lieutenant Jeff Niiya, who even warned Patriot Prayer brawler Tusitala "Tiny" Toese to skip protests to avoid being arrested on an active warrant.[18]

As the right wing's bogeyman du jour shifted from Black Lives Matter's "terrorists" to antifa "communists," Gibson endeavored to build national prominence and support through constant antagonistic demonstrations. Gibson's praxis is reflective of the growing right-wing politics of classic urban revanchism that views cities as debauched liberal havens overrun by people of color, transpeople, the poor, atheists, and immigrants who must be brought in line.

As evidence of the deepening urban and rural divide, the Republican Party lost its last urban congressional district anywhere in the country in the 2018 rout.[19] Under Trump, the federal government has taken an increasingly hostile approach to growing urban autonomy, for example by threatening sanctions against sanctuary cities.

In August 2018, in response to the mass detention of immigrants in camps and the deaths of several children, Occupy ICE protests began to sweep the country. Originating in Portland, these protests popularized a call for the abolition of Immigration and Customs Enforcement. In response, Trump issued a statement criticizing Portland's mayor for "shamefully ordering local police to stand down" and leaving federal law enforcement to "face an angry mob of violent people." Soon afterward—and ahead of the August 17, 2019 End Domestic Terrorism rally organized by Infowars contributor Mike Biggs, leader of the hate group Proud Boys—Trump again weighed in with support for the group by tweeting,

Under Trump, the federal government has taken an increasingly hostile approach to growing urban autonomy.

17 Katie Shepherd, "Portland Police Chief Says Protesters Went Off to 'Whine and Complain' Last Week Because Officers 'Kicked Your Butt,'" *Willamette Week*, August 15, 2018, www.wweek.com/news/courts/2018/08/15/portland-police-chief-says-protesters-went-off-to-whine-and-complain-last-week-because-officers-kicked-your-butt/.

18 Katie Shepherd, "Texts Between Portland Police and Patriot Prayer Ringleader Joey Gibson Show Warm Exchange," *Willamette Week*, February 14, 2019, www.wweek.com/news/courts/2019/02/14/texts-between-portland-police-and-patriot-prayer-ringleader-joey-gibson-show-warm-exchange/.

19 Luiz, Romero, "Republicans Lost Their Last Urban District Last Night," *Quartz*, November 7, 2018, qz.com/1454293/republicans-lost-their-last-urban-district-in-the-us-last-night/.

"Major consideration is being given to naming ANTIFA an 'ORGANIZATION OF TERROR.' Portland is being watched very closely. Hopefully the Mayor will be able to properly do his job!"[20]

As urban centers become the backbone of a growing leftist movement in the United States and the site of support for increasingly progressive candidates and legislation, we are likely to continue to see heavy backing for right wing urban revanchist movements on behalf of extractive industry executives and urban bourgeoisie interested in undermining the growing number of people unwilling to sit idly by as the world burns and kids are put in cages.

Despite Portland's manufactured reputation as a liberal utopia, these struggles prefigure a more dynamic and accurate image of the city.

In the Ashes, A Fertile Ecology of Resistance

Portland's racist history is matched by a historical countercurrent of liberationist social movements that have adapted in the face of enormous challenges. In the uncertain future that is to come, it is only the strength of our communities, our interconnectedness, and the regular practice of struggle that will allow us to pass down the lessons of how to cooperate in resistance. As I have argued elsewhere, much of the growth of resistance movements in the city has been the result of a developmental movement against white supremacy, which owes its origins to the civil rights movement.

In 2018, Portland again set national resistance precedent by launching the Occupy ICE movement, calling for the abolition of the agency and conducting a weeks-long siege of ICE headquarters in the barricaded autonomous zone known as Camp Multnomah.

Despite Portland's manufactured reputation as a liberal utopia, these struggles prefigure a more dynamic and accurate image of the city, as its history of social and economic inequality, violent racism, and resistance to these tyrannies re-erupts. While we have seen this cycle for decades, what is new is that more Portlanders on the margins of power are uniting to fight back against systemic

---

20 Donald J. Trump, @realDonaldTrump, Twitter, August 17, 2019, https://twitter.com/realDonaldTrump/status/1162726857231544320.

oppression and to co-create and model an inclusive society. It is only the lineage of perennial struggle that has transformed Portland from a racist backwater to a place where radical political and social culture shine through and create the hope of equality. Portlantifa is here to stay. ◄

Photo Credits